K It Up!

A Guide to the Gross, the Bad, and the Smelly

Megan McDonald illustrated by Peter H. Reynolds

CANDLEWICK PRESS

CONTENTS

Get Your Stink On!

Have you ever been slimed by an elephant booger the size of a basketball? Or fainted from the fumes of a 100-pound glob of whale vomit? Have you ever dined on hedgehog at a Roadkill Café or whipped up a whopping batch of reindeer poop? Sniff out all the facts here—the gross, the bad, and the smelly. All you have to do is turn the page . . . if you dare. No raincoat needed!

You've Been Skunked!

A book about stinky things has to start with the most famous smelly creature of all, don't you think? That would be—what else?— the skunk! Get a whiff of these skunk facts:

* A bunch of skunks is called a stench. P.U.!

* The word *skunk* comes from the Algonquian word *seganku,* which comes from the words for "to urinate" and "fox."

DID YOU KNOW?

The scientific name for skunk is *Mephitis mephitis*, which means "noxious gas, noxious gas." (It's so stinky, they had to say it twice!)

✳ Skunks have a secret smelly weapon when they sense danger: skunk spray! The foul-smelling, stinging chemicals squirt out of scent glands on their rear end, smelling like rotten eggs, garlic, and burnt rubber.

✳ Skunks eat bees! A hungry skunk will scarf down bees one by one as they come out of their hive. Yum, yum!

GARLIC

3

＊ Before spraying an enemy or predator, a skunk will first raise its tail as a warning. Then it will stomp its feet. The spotted skunk will even try to freak out a predator by doing a handstand. If that doesn't work, the skunk will *hisssss!* If all else fails—*ppppppsssssshhhhh!*—you've been skunked.

Get Away from Me!

While the skunk uses spray to keep danger away, these creatures have other clever ways of saying "Back off!"

Hairy Frog or Horror Frog?

Like something out of a horror movie, the hairy frog can use its own skeleton to scare off predators. When it's under attack, this freaky frog can break its own toe bones—which then stick out of its skin like claws. Yikes!

6

Snap . . . Crackle . . . POP!

Look out—here comes the bombardier beetle, with its built-in stink bomb. When this beetle is threatened, it mixes two chemicals in its abdomen, which then heat up to a boil and explode with a loud *pop!* The beetle can spray twenty-nine times in a row!

It's ~~Not~~ Nice to Fool Mother Nature

The monarch butterfly feeds on poisonous plants so it will taste yucky if a predator tries to eat it.

Your Breath Is Killing Me!

Maybe you can't spray your enemies like a skunk can, but you can always try breathing on them! Meanwhile, take a breather with this quiz:

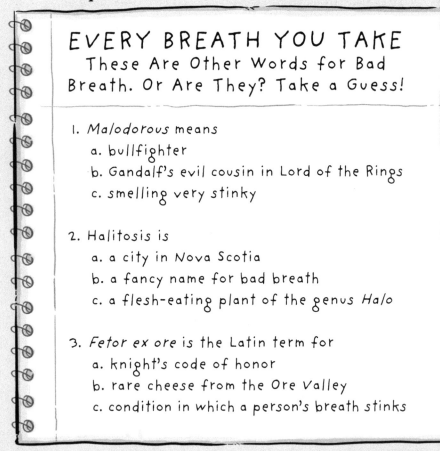

EVERY BREATH YOU TAKE
These Are Other Words for Bad Breath. Or Are They? Take a Guess!

1. *Malodorous* means
    a. bullfighter
    b. Gandalf's evil cousin in Lord of the Rings
    c. smelling very stinky

2. *Halitosis* is
    a. a city in Nova Scotia
    b. a fancy name for bad breath
    c. a flesh-eating plant of the genus *Halo*

3. *Fetor ex ore* is the Latin term for
    a. knight's code of honor
    b. rare cheese from the Ore Valley
    c. condition in which a person's breath stinks

4. Which of these are NOT real cures
   for bad breath?
   a. brushing your teeth
   b. sleeping with garlic under your pillow
   c. flossing your teeth
   d. scraping your tongue with a spoon
   e. singing the Alphabet Song
   f. standing on your head
   g. chewing gum
   h. eating cinnamon
   i. drinking more water
   j. writing a letter to the Tooth Fairy

5. Which of these things are known to
   cause bad breath?
   a. drinking coffee
   b. smoking
   c. eating onions
   d. eating garlic
   e. gum disease
   f. sleeping with your mouth open
   g. skipping breakfast
   h. all of the above

Turn to page 119 for the answers.

Full of Hot Air? Then Burp!

When you swallow food, if small amounts of air get swallowed along with it, the air will later escape through your mouth as a burp.

DID YOU KNOW?

A gorilla burps when it is upset or annoyed.

* Animal burps and farts release 80 million tons of methane gas into the atmosphere each year.

* Doctors call burping eructation.

* An Englishman named Paul Hunn can burp a whopping 109.9 decibels. That's as loud as a chain saw. Some people claim that it's possible to burp at 170 decibels. That's as loud as a fighter jet!

* In some places, such as Bahrain, it is polite to burp after a meal. It means you enjoyed the food!

HOW TO ANNOY YOUR SISTER IN JUST ONE BURP

Try this:
1. Stand or sit up straight (gas rises).
2. Drink a glass of carbonated water with no ice.
3. When you feel the bubbles start to rise, open wide and let 'er rip!

DID YOU KNOW?

A farp is when you burp and fart at the same time.

Excellent Expectorating!

(Expectorate is a fancy word for spit.)

* Spitting might be gross, but a hundred years ago, it was way cool. Every fancy home, including the White House, had a spittoon. Back then, lots of people chewed tobacco and needed a place to spit it out. Eeuw!

DID YOU KNOW?

A loogie is a gross wad of spit mixed with snot!

* Your body will make 5,000 gallons of spit in your lifetime. That's enough to fill a small swimming pool!

HOW TO MAKE A
PERFECT SPITBALL

You will need:
- Some paper
- A straw
- Some spit

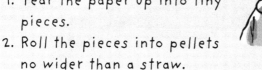

1. Tear the paper up into tiny pieces.
2. Roll the pieces into pellets no wider than a straw.
3. Wet the paper balls in your mouth.
4. Load a ball into the straw at the end near your mouth.
5. Blow the wet ball through the straw at your target. *P-tooey!*

Tips:
- Remember not to breathe in once you've loaded the straw.
- Try not to let anyone see you do it.
- Stockpile several spitballs before you shoot.
- Do not aim for anyone's face. The back of the head works great!

Up Your Nose

ACHOO!

Astro Boogers!

Ever been hit by a meteorite? Maybe . . .
if you've ever been sneezed on! Boogers are
made up of stuff we breathe in through
our noses, which is anything that might
be floating in the air—pollen, dust, dirt,
even space dust. Think about it—the next
time somebody sneezes, there just might/
maybe/could be a teeny-tiny piece of
meteorite in the snot that flies. Cosmic!

Big Boogies!

It's snot funny . . . An elephant booger is as big as a basketball. No lie!

bless you...

Annual Booger Shootout

At the Red Lion pub in England, Gale Hollingsworth became the first woman to win the Annual Booger Shooting Contest. In a move called a farmer's blow, she held one nostril closed and blew a booger out the other nostril. It sailed clear across the room, almost 20 feet! *THWAP!* That booger stuck to the wall.

ACHOOOO!!

Get Out the Rain Slicker

Human sneezes
exit at around 40 miles per hour.
Super hachoo-er Reginald Kaulman's
honkers have been clocked at an
astonishing 175 miles per hour.

The Big Sneeze

Whales sneeze at 300 miles per hour—that's
the power of a class-five hurricane and as
fast as a tornado. *Bless you!*

15 ft.

Once Upon a Slime

* From ancient Greece to the Middle Ages, snail slime was used in cough syrup.

* Snail slime is now used in anti-aging skin lotions and creams.

* Slug slime has been used to treat warts and zits.

* The stinkhorn is a mushroom with a pink head covered in yucky-blucky brown slime. The slime smells like rotting meat or sewage. Smell ya later!

✳ Hagfish are also known as slime eels. They secrete ooey, gooey slime that helps them tie themselves in a knot if captured.

✳ To play dead, an opossum will roll over on its side, hang its tongue out of its mouth, and drool out a green slime that smells like rotting flesh.

* Who spit in my soup? Most likely, it was a bird called a swiftlet. Their nests, which are made of spit, are collected to make a Chinese dish called bird's nest soup! Nests are collected from caves, and a kilogram's worth can fetch up to $10,000.

21

* Do not annoy a camel. If you do, it will likely slime you with its special brand of spit, made of juice from its stomach mixed with saliva. *Pass the towel, please!*

WHICH SLIMEBALL
SAID WHAT?

1. The Slimer
   (from *Ghostbusters*)

2. Slimey the Worm
   (from *Sesame Street*)

3. Bartholomew
   (from *Bartholomew and
   the Oobleck* by Dr. Seuss)

4. Jabba the Hutt
   (from the Star Wars movies)

5. The Slime Mutant
   (from *Scooby-Doo*)

6. The Blob
   (from the *X-Men* comic books)

7. Homer Simpson
   (from *The Simpsons*)

a. "Let me have a lick
   at you!"

b. "Boonowa tweepi,
   ha, ha."

c. "Beware the beast
   from below."

d. "It's gummy! It's like
   glue!"

e. "Did you just call me
   'blob'?"

f. "My greatest fear is
   broccoli."

g. "Slimey to the
   moon!"

Turn to page 119 for the answers.

Dirty Disasters

Talk About Fast Food!

In 126 BC, Mount Etna, a volcano in
Sicily, blew its lid. Lava flowed into the
Ionian Sea, boiling the water and cooking
thousands of fish. Sadly, people
who ate the fish later died.

The Case of the Exploding Sauerkraut

Special teams trained to handle dangerous
substances suited up to inspect a high
school in British Columbia after a can of
sauerkraut exploded on students during
a science experiment. No food poisoning
was discovered—some say the can "farted"
from fermentation.

Ka-POOP!

On Friday the 13th in 1981, two women in Louisville, Kentucky, were on their way to work when a spark from their car touched off a gigantic sewer explosion. Sinkhole city! The town was super stinky for almost two years while crews worked to repair the sewer system.

Sludge Fest

In 2008 in Kingston, Tennessee, a dam broke, releasing a whopping 1.1 billion gallons of yucky, blucky sticky sludge from a coal plant's outflow into branches of the Tennessee River.

Putrid Places

Have you ever been to Stink City? Here are some smelly burgs sure to curl your nose hairs:

Clothespin Time!

In Hereford, Texas, there are 241 cows for every person. That's a lotta cow plop. Better hold your nose!

Hold the Cherry!

Cherries may taste good, but they sure don't smell good when they're being made into maraschino cherries. The wastewater from making these cherries stinks up the town of Williamsburg, Michigan, making it smell like dead deer.

Musée des Égouts de Paris
(The Paris Sewer Museum)

Hold your nose and head underground to tour the actual sewers of Paris!

Stinky Town

Rotorua, New Zealand, calls itself the Stink Capital of the World. If you like the smell of rotten eggs, you've come to the right place. Gushing geysers, mineral lakes, and mud baths earned the town its nickname of Sulphur City.

The Scoop on Poop

Chew, chew, chew. Here comes Number Two! Doo-doo. Dung. Plop. Turds. . . . Food moves through your digestive tract. Any parts of the food that your body doesn't use comes out the other end. You got poop!

* By the time you grow up, your intestines will be 25 feet long. (A horse's intestines are 89 feet long.)

* Your intestines will process 100,000 pounds of food in your lifetime. That's 50 tons, or the weight of 25 SUVs.

Whooo's Hungry for Some Poop?

DID YOU KNOW?

In olden times, doctors used to taste a patient's poop to try to figure out what was making the person sick!

The burrowing owl uses a piece of poop to lure dung beetles into its lair. *Gulp!* Bye-bye, beetles.

Your Breath Smells Poopy Fresh!

In India, cows are sacred, so Indians don't think cow poop and pee are yucky. Each cow in India produces 32,000 pounds of dung per year, and some of those droppings are used as fuel, in building houses, and even in toothpaste. *Mmm-mmm,* poopalicious!

Got Gloves?

Guess where the world's highest-priced coffee beans can be found. You got it. In poop! The Asian palm civet, a small, catlike mammal, loves to eat coffee berries. It digests the berries' fleshy pulp and poops out the beans. Farmers then wash, dry, and roast them. The beans' trip through the civet's digestive system is said to remove acids and make for a smooth cuppa Joe.

Stinky Tea

In China, *wu ling zhi*—flying-squirrel dung—is made into a hot tea, and used to treat snake bites and other ailments.

Pretty Far-out Poop

Inside caves in Hawaii, scientists have found lava tubes that drip with a blue-green ooze. It looks like a mineral, but it's actually the poop of tiny organisms called microbes. Similar caves have been discovered on Mars, too. So just think—this mini-poop could point the way to finding life on Mars!

Satellite Scat

Scientists study penguin poop from space! Satellite images of the poop from a colony of Emperor penguins provide researchers with clues to the penguins' health, population, and response to climate change.

ALL THIS TALK OF POOP MAKING YOU HUNGRY?

Then whip up some tasty poop for Christmas!

Here's a no-bake recipe for Reindeer Poop:

- 3 cups oats
- 6 tablespoons cocoa powder
- 3½ ounces coconut flakes
- ¼ pound butter (1 stick)
- 1 cup sugar
- ½ cup milk
- 1 teaspoon vanilla

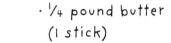

1. Mix the oats, cocoa powder, and coconut in a bowl.
2. Ask a grown-up to help melt the butter in a saucepan, then mix in the sugar and milk.
3. Remove the pan from the heat, and add the vanilla.
4. Pour the milk mixture into the oats mixture and mix well.
5. Scoop heaping teaspoons of the final mixture onto waxed paper.
6. Let it cool. *Voilà!* Reindeer poop for all.

Have a hankering for dung
but no time to cook?

Some quick and easy ideas:

- Mini marshmallows make great snowman droppings.
- Chocolate-covered raisins can double for penguin poop.
- Brownie bites look like polar-bear poop.

Put any of these in a small plastic bag.
Tie a ribbon on it. Make a funny label.
Amaze your friends!

DID YOU KNOW?

Coprophagia is the scientific name for poop eating!

A Brief History of the Diaper

Sniff, sniff. What's that smell? For as long as babies have peed and pooped, there have been dirty diapers. But they weren't always plastic-coated and pulled from a box.

DID YOU KNOW?

Shakespeare was the first to call a diaper a diaper. In the U.S., the word stuck. But the Brits prefer to call them nappies.

Here's what diapers were made of
since way back when:

Ancient times	Sealskin, rabbit skin, milkweed leaves, moss, grass
1800s	Linen, cotton
1900s	Cotton
1960s	Throwaway diapers made of plastics
2000s	Return of the cloth diaper

Peep! Peep! Poop!

Bertha Dlugi of Milwaukee, Wisconsin, earned patent number 2,882,858 for her invention—a diaper for parakeets.

I see London, I see France

Move over, tighty whities. Get a load of these underpants:

The most expensive set of ladies underwear ever sold cost $15 million. They were sewn with rubies and diamonds!

Going on safari? Pack some paper undies, the latest thing in travel. Great for hiking and camping, too. Or even a wedgie gone wild! Chuck 'em, bury 'em, or . . . recycle 'em? P.U.!

How would you like to have underwear named after you? Long johns are named after the famous boxer John L. Sullivan because he boxed in long-undie-type pants.

Recycle your holey, old undies. (CLEAN only, puh-lease!) They get shredded, reused, and someday could end up as the stuffing in your couch or car seat!

In Minnesota, a law says you are not allowed to hang boy undies next to girl undies on the clothesline.

In Thailand, it's illegal to leave your home if you're not wearing underwear.

Don't wash that car! With undies, that is. In California, it's against the law to use dirty undies as a rag.

It's NOT against the law to wear 215 pairs of undies at one time! In fact, on June 13, 2010, ten-year-old Jack Singer of New York did so to break the previous record— a mere 200 pairs.

Mummies

Don't want to be a rotting corpse? Be a
mummy! In ancient times, mummies
were made to preserve bodies of humans
and animals from rotting, stinking decay.
After all, you want to look your best in the
afterlife!

HOW TO MAKE A MUMMY
IN TEN EASY STEPS

1. Pull out the guts and put the lungs, stomach, intestines, and liver in their own special jars.
2. Pull the brain out through the nose.
3. Toss the other organs (except the heart).
4. Soak the body in natron (a kind of salt) for forty days.
5. Rub oil on the dried-out skin.
6. Stuff the insides with sand, sawdust, or spices.
7. Wrap the body in linen strips, starting with the toes and fingers.
8. Place a special object, amulet, or good-luck charm every few layers.
9. Sing special chants over the body.
10. Use tree resin (sap) to keep the linen strips in place.

Who's Your Mummy?

Before you unwrap that baby-size mummy, be prepared for a little surprise! You might find the body of a hawk or bird of prey, wrapped with so many bandages that they wound up looking about the same size as a baby. And they wore human masks to boot! Peek-a-boo!

Here Lies Mittens

Over one million animal mummies have been found in Egypt—dogs, apes, ibises, even hippos. Many animal mummies were cats, because cats were sacred. They were thought to represent the goddess Bastet. Cats often had their own tombs and were buried with their favorite toy: you guessed it—a mouse mummy.

Mummy Medicine

In ancient times, it was believed that if you ground up mummies and ate the mummy dust, you would be cured of yucky diseases. *Rx: Take two bites of mummy, and call me in the morning.*

DID YOU KNOW?

The oldest mummy in North America, found in a cave in Nevada, is more than nine thousand years old!

PARTY MUMMY

For your next birthday party,
try something new. How about
a toilet-paper mummy-wrapping
game?

You will need:
- Two teams with 3 players each
- 4 rolls of toilet paper
- 2 rolls of masking tape

1. Each team gets two rolls of toilet paper
   and one roll of tape. Choose your mummy.
   The other two players are the wrappers.
2. Starting at the ankles, begin unwinding
   the toilet paper. Wrap it around and
   around the mummy. Do not cover the
   person's feet, mouth, or eyes.
3. Give the teams a time limit of 5–10
   minutes.

Wrap and roll. May the best mummy win!

Revolting History

History stinks! A few smelly blasts from the past:

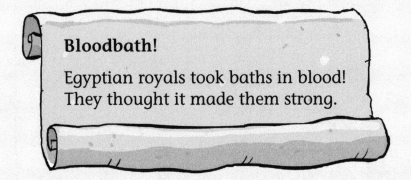

Bloodbath!

Egyptian royals took baths in blood! They thought it made them strong.

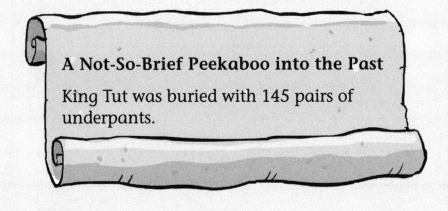

A Not-So-Brief Peekaboo into the Past

King Tut was buried with 145 pairs of underpants.

Too Big for His Britches

King Henry VIII was huge when he died and was buried in a lead coffin. One day soon after, the coffin burst open, and blood and guts shot out. The bloated corpse had exploded!

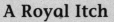

A Royal Itch

They say King James I never had a bath in his life. Pee-uuey! He had special slits in his clothing for scratching at his fleas.

A Pox upon You!

For as long as there have been people, there have been ucky, blucky diseases.

The top three killers:

- Smallpox (430 BC): killed more than 300 million people.

- The Spanish flu (1918–1919): killed as many as 100 million people.

- The Black Death, aka the bubonic plague (1300s): killed 25 million people.

Flea-Bitten

The plague was spread by fleas.

Here are some surefire ways that people in the Dark Ages tried to get rid of fleas:

- They covered their clothes with pig grease.

- They spread cow poop all over their floors.

- They hung splinters from a tree struck by lightning around their necks.

    Think any of them worked?

Cooties

It all started in World War I, when soldiers wrote about lice, bugs, and rats in the trenches and called any pests cooties. They were also called arithmetic bugs, because they "added" trouble. To get rid of cooties, soldiers took pickle baths.

Book Cooties

The word started among soldiers as slang for icky pests like lice. Then one day *cooties* started popping up in kids' books.

Check out Eleanor Estes's *Ginger Pye* (1951) and Beverly Cleary's *Mitch and Amy* (1967). Can you find the word *cooties*?

Turn to page 119 for hints.

If the pickle bath doesn't work, try this:

Draw a circle on your arm two times.
Now poke the middle of the circle two
times and say:
   Circle, circle, dot, dot,
   Now you've got
   the cootie shot!

GOT COOTIES?

The game of Cooties, that is. (In the U.K., it's called Beetle.) You play by rolling a die and drawing an ugly bug step by step.

To play:

For each roll of the die, draw a part of the bug (see chart). You must first roll a 6 and start with the bug's body. You must also roll a 5 for the head before you can draw the antennae and eyes. The first person to complete his or her bug yells, "Cooties!"

- · 6 Body
- · 5 Head
- · 4 Wings (two)
- · 3 Legs (six)
- · 2 Antennae (two)
- · 1 Eyes (two)

(Must draw body before anything else. Must draw head before eyes and antennae.)

Frankenstein's Creature Lab

THE EXQUISITE CORPSE

In the early 1900s, a drawing game called the Exquisite Corpse became popular. Create a cartoon creature with your friends!

Here's how to play:
1. Fold a blank sheet of paper in half. Now fold it in half again.
2. Unfold. On the top section of the creased paper, draw a head and neck.
3. Fold the section back so the drawing is hidden, and pass the paper to a friend. Ask him or her to draw a body on the next section of the paper (shoulders, arms, and torso).
4. Fold that back and pass the paper on. The next person draws the hips, thighs, and knees.
5. Fold it back and pass it on. The next person draws legs and feet.
6. Unfold to reveal your crazy creature!

Make your creature kooky! Try these wacky ideas:

- Robot arms
- Alien head
- Insect legs
- Zombie brain
- Belly button middle
- Tree trunk
- Frog feet

A group of famous children's book authors wrote an Exquisite Corpse tale, passing the story along chapter by chapter. Read the whole book, called *The Exquisite Corpse Adventure*, published by Candlewick Press.

Not at All A-Peeling

Skin holds us in. It protects our insides. Don't want your organs spilling out, do you? It also sends important signals to our brain (Don't touch that hot stove!), helps with our sense of touch (kitten = soft, sandpaper = rough), and helps us heal (think *scabs*!).

I'm Falling Apart!

- Thirty to forty thousand dead skin cells fall from your body every single minute! In just one month, your body has made a whole new layer of skin.

- You will shed 40 pounds of skin in your lifetime.

- Combine dead skin with dirt and oil, and you've got dandruff.

- Dust bunnies! More than half the dust in your house is made of dead skin cells.

Fuzzy Navel

Graham Barker holds the world record for the largest collection of belly-button lint. He has been collecting it since 1984.

Georg Steinhauser, an Austrian chemist, studied belly-button lint for three years. What did he learn after all that? That hairy tummies make more BBL (belly-button lint) than tummies that aren't hairy.

Other things we now know to be true:

○ Males have more BBL than females.

○ On average, an innie belly button collects 2.03 milligrams of BBL per day. Outies don't collect much BBL at all.

Smelly Belly Button?

P.U. Does your belly button smell like cheese? You might have a rare disease called *stinkalobelia*. Just kidding. Belly buttons collect dead skin cells, sweat, and clothing lint. You probably just forgot to wash it out the last time you took a bath.

Peanut Butter and Toe Jam

Toe jam is like belly-button lint between your toes. Toe cheese is a green fungus that grows between the toes from not changing your socks for days . . . and days.

Gross meter: 10

Many frogs, salamanders, and lizards, especially geckos, shed their skin and *eat it*! It's full of calcium. Yum!

Gross meter: 5

A snake rubs against something rough to tear a hole in its old skin. As it crawls out, its skin turns inside out, as if the snake were taking off a sock. Birds use the old skin to line their nests.

Gross meter: 8

A land hermit crab
will bury itself for
weeks while it molts and eats its old shell.

Gross meter: 4

As a bedbug grows, it will shed
its skin five times.

Gross meter: 7

In traditional Chinese medicine, dried
casings of cicadas are used to cure poison
ivy and other itchy rashes.

Are You Going to Eat That?

Here's the poop on animals. They sure do eat some crazy-weird stuff!

Dung Diners

* Puffins eat whale dung.

* Ivory gulls eat polar-bear poop.

* Dogs love to eat cat poop because it's high in protein.

* Rabbits, rodents, and gorillas, as well as many insects and other plant eaters will eat their own poop! Because what they eat is hard to digest, they have to eat it twice! Poop has lots of vitamins.

Do I Look Fat in This?

* Every night, vampire bats drink half their body weight in blood.

* Guess what happened when a Burmese python (a whopping 13-footer) swallowed an alligator whole? *Ka-boom!* It exploded. Snake guts + gator guts = eeuw stew!

* Caterpillars eat 27,000 times their body weight.

Oh, Baby!

The spadefoot toad eats its own tadpoles.

Mr. Sandman

There are moths in Asia that eat the eye gunk of cattle, buffalo, and elephants.

Watch Your Step!

The plover picks out bits of food to eat from between the teeth of a crocodile!

Rat Snacks

Rats will eat just about anything—paint, leather, even an elephant's toenail!

Beauty and the Feet

Butterflies will sip at sweaty sneakers to get salt.

Weird Eats

Get your bib on for some of the strangest things ever eaten!

TODAY'S SPECIALS!

Weird stuff people have eaten:
true or false?

bicycle T/F	lightbulbs T/F	soap T/F
birch tree T/F	rocks T/F	mud T/F
coins T/F	buttons T/F	a couch T/F

Turn to page 119 for the answers.

Stop That Thief!

Simon Hooper saw the ring he wanted to give his girlfriend, but it cost too much. So he ate it! Dorchester, England, police caught him by running a metal detector over his tummy. He went to jail for three days until he pooped out the ring!

The Big Cheese

Q: What's big and yellow, weighs 1,400 pounds, and made a big stink at the White House in 1837?

A: Cheese! President Andrew Jackson's favorite food. In 1835, a cheesemaker sent a giant 1,400-pound wheel of cheddar to the White House. For two years, Jackson ate the cheese and gave it to friends. On leaving office two years later, he still hadn't finished the cheese. So he held a big party and brought out the seriously smelly old cheese. It was so stinky that some people fainted. Ten thousand people came to the party and ate it in two hours! After the party, the carpet was slippery with cheese glop. Cheese skating, anyone?

Just Scraped from the Road

In the U.S., Canada, the U.K., and some other countries, there are people who eat roadkill. No lie.

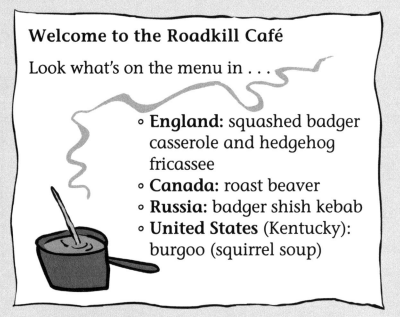

Welcome to the Roadkill Café

Look what's on the menu in . . .

- **England:** squashed badger casserole and hedgehog fricassee
- **Canada:** roast beaver
- **Russia:** badger shish kebab
- **United States** (Kentucky): burgoo (squirrel soup)

From deer, moose, bear, and elk that are hit by cars, to armadillos, raccoons, skunks, and birds, they'll throw them in the pot! There's even a cookbook with recipes for cooking roadkill. Moose meatballs, anyone?

SING A SONG OF ROADKILL
(Sung to the tune of "Three Blind Mice")

Roadkill stew
Roadkill stew
Tastes so good
Just like it should.

First you go down to the interstate
You wait for the critter to meet its fate
You take it home and you make it great

Roadkill stew
Roadkill stew

VOMITOCIOUS AWARD

What is the grossest food in the world? You be the judge. Vote for the (real) food that grosses you out the most!

○ **Maggot Cheese** *(Sardinia)*
Yep, that's cheese crawling with worms. Take goat's milk. Add larvae of flies. Let flies hatch and feed on cheese. Time to eat—flies and all!

○ **Stink Heads** *(Alaska)*
Chop off a salmon head. Bury it in the ground for three weeks. Dig it up. Mash it up. Serve cold like pudding!

◯ **Jellied Moose Nose** *(Alaska)*
Chop off moose's nose. Boil it till the hairs
come off. Add spice. Slice and serve cold.
Don't forget the garlic!

◯ **Bat Soup** *(Asia)*
Take one live bat. Drop it into a pot of
boiling milk. Mix and mash herbs and
spices. Start sipping!

◯ **Hasma** *(China)*
Take dried, shrunken frog organs.
Just add water! A bit of sugar
makes this a yummy dessert.

What's Up, Chuck?

Upchuck. Puke. Hurl. Barf. Toss a sidewalk pizza. No matter what you call it, it's not pretty. It's vomit-ocious!

Spilling Your Guts

Did you know that frogs throw up? They puke their guts out. No lie. It was discovered on a space mission that a frog throws up its stomach first. The frog digs out all of the stomach's contents, then swallows the stomach back down again!

Lick . . . Lick . . . Gulp

Does your cat have a trichobezoar? Relax—it's just a slimy hair ball. Cats swallow hair from grooming themselves, then spit it back up.

Dinosaur Puke?

The 160-million-year-old fossilized vomit of an ichthyosaur was discovered in 2002 in Peterborough, England.

Puke Overboard!

Ambergris is a fancy name for whale vomit. When whales can't digest everything they eat, they throw up a 100-pound slimeball that smells like poop. Oddly enough, its main use is in perfumes.

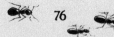

No Puking at the Table, Please!

In Roman times, people ate so much that is was common to puke after dinner. Get thee to the vomitorium, a special room just for puking.

Gross Grub Menu

Snap, crackle, pop! All over the world, people eat insects for protein, from grubs and grasshoppers to tarantulas and termites. Check out this creepy-crawly menu. *Mmm-mmm, good.*

Appetizers

* Grilled black witch moths
* Leaf-footed bug salsa with roasted mealworms
* Deep-fried crickets

Soup & Salad

* Wasp salad
* Soup with boll-weevil croutons

Main Dishes

* Mealworm spaghetti
* Stinkbug pizza
* Chop suey ants
* Dragonfly kebab
* Grasshopper enchiladas

Desserts

* Honeypot ants
* Chocolate-covered locusts
* Chocolate-chip mealworm cookies
* Cricket fruitcake

Don't forget to
drink your milk.
Roach milk, that is.

MEALWORM SPAGHETTI

- 1 tablespoon safflower oil
- 1/4 teaspoon salt
- 1 sprig marjoram
- 1 sprig thyme
- 2 bay leaves
- 1/4 onion, chopped
- 8 ounces dry spaghetti
- 6 to 8 tablespoons butter
- 1/2 pound purple basil, finely chopped
- 10 sprigs parsley, finely chopped
- 1/2 pound ricotta cheese
- 2 tablespoons olive oil
- 3 to 4 tablespoons pine nuts, finely chopped
- 1/2 pound roasted yellow mealworms
- 1/4 cup whole pine nuts

1. Bring 4 1/2 cups water to a boil. Add the safflower oil, salt, marjoram, thyme, bay leaves, and onion.
2. Add the spaghetti. Drain when done.
3. Melt the butter in a saucepan. Add the spaghetti. Mix in the basil, parsley, ricotta, olive oil, and chopped pine nuts with the spaghetti. Heat but do not boil.
4. Top with the mealworms and pine nuts.

DID YOU KNOW?

There are 1,462 types of edible insects.

If you get the bug to eat a bug, try finding a bug or bug-eating festival near you:

The Bug Bowl

Purdue University
West Lafayette, IN
Complete with a cricket-spitting contest!

Bug Chef Cook-Off

Broad Appétit Food Festival
Richmond, VA
White-chocolate waxworm cookies, anyone?

Bug Day

Randall Museum
San Francisco, CA
Author Megan McDonald ate a roasted cricket and a toasted mealworm here. No lie!

Bugfest

Smithsonian Museum of Natural History
Washington, D.C.
*Don't miss the
hissing-cockroach
races!*

The Insectarium

Philadelphia, PA
*Try a tasty mealworm at the
museum's traveling show.*

Icky Insects

Meet some creepy crawlies of the six-legged variety. These guys are sure to make your skin crawl!

Wigged Out!

It was once thought that earwigs could crawl in your ear and tunnel into your brain while you're sleeping. That's how they got their name, but it's not true. Earwig fossils date back to the Late Triassic period.

85

Dung Beetles

Dung beetles feed on poop!

There are three kinds of dung beetles:

- Rollers roll the poop into a big ball and take it home to eat later.

- Tunnelers bury the dung for safekeeping.

- Dwellers set up house in the dung and slowly munch on their home.

* Dung beetles live on every continent except Antarctica.

* When dung beetles are rolling dung into a ball, they will follow a straight line no matter what obstacles are in their path. Any they have to roll fast, or another beetle might steal their dinner!

* Dried dung beetles are used in traditional Chinese medicine to cure ten different diseases.

Cockroaches

Ken Edwards ate thirty-six cockroaches in one minute on the set of *The Big Breakfast* in London on March 5, 2001.

✳ What has no wings but can scale smooth glass? What has horns and makes a hissing sound when it fights? Move over, Superman. It's the Hisser! The Madagascar hissing cockroach, that is.

TEST YOUR COCKROACH KNOW-HOW:

1. In Australia's annual
   Cockroach Racing
   Championship, the
   winning roach scores
   a prize of:
   a. a book of stamps
      with glue—yum!
   b. $500
   c. a bar of soap

2. How many knees
   does a cockroach
   have?
   a. zero
   b. twelve
   c. eighteen

3. A cockroach can
   hold its breath for:
   a. forty minutes
   b. three days
   c. up to one week

4. What color is a
   cockroach's blood?
   a. vampire red
   b. mud brown
   c. ghost white

5. A crushed cockroach
   can be used as:
   a. chewing gum
   b. a Band-Aid
   c. a cooking spice

6. A cockroach can live
   without eating for:
   a. a day
   b. a year
   c. a month

Turn to page 119
for the answers.

Food Most Foul

Guess what's coming to dinner? Bugs and rodent hairs! You heard it right. The FDA inspects food to make it safe. But did you know certain creepy-crawlies wiggle their way in? The FDA says it's okay to have a small amount of rodent hairs, droppings, and insect parts in our food.

* Canned tomatoes: 10 fly eggs per 2 cups

* Macaroni: 225 insect parts per cup

* Mushrooms: 20 maggots per half cup

* Peanut butter: 1 rat hair and 30 insect parts per half cup

* Popcorn: 2 rodent hairs or 1 rodent turd per pound

* Potato chips: 6 percent of potatoes are allowed to be rotten

* Spices: 325 insect parts per 5 teaspoons

* Wheat flour: 75 insect pieces per quarter cup

A Load of Rubbish

Heave-ho! Americans toss out a whopping 250 million tons of trash each year. That means every person in the U.S. throws away almost 4½ pounds of garbage per day.

The Pits

It once was a copper mine known as the Richest Hill in the World. Today, just outside Butte, Montana, lies the Pit of Life and Death—a toxic pit of green poison a mile and a half wide and a third of a mile deep. No plants grow there, no insects buzz there, and no fish swim there. The only thing that can survive there is a slime called *Euglena mutabilis*.

What a Dump!

Out in the middle of the ocean is a swirling, whirling island of garbage called the Great Pacific Garbage Patch. Plastic bags and bottles, tires, lawn chairs, flip-flops, hockey gloves, computer monitors, and even rubber duckies are just a few of the items that make up a garbage cesspool the size of Texas.

Zombie-fied

There are 405 dead zones in the world's oceans. Nothing can live in these areas because the deep water there doesn't have enough oxygen due to man-made chemicals. The largest dead zone near the U.S. is the size of New Jersey and stretches off the coast in the Gulf of Mexico.

That's Ducky!

In 1992, 28,000 rubber ducks (as well as plastic frogs, beavers, and turtles) washed overboard from a cargo ship in the Pacific. Twenty years later, some are still found floating as far away as Hawaii to Iceland to Australia.

Where Have All the Trash Trucks Gone?

Garbage collectors stopped picking up trash in Naples, Italy, in December 2007 and didn't get back to work until the middle of January 2008. By then, the city was overflowing with a month's worth of garbage. P. Ueey!

Trash to Treasure

Mount Trashmore in Virginia Beach is a mountain 60 feet high and 800 feet long that was created from garbage. Layers of garbage and soil were compacted to build what is now a popular park.

Mushy History Mystery

When museum officials in Pittsburgh dug up a time capsule after a hundred years . . . it stank! Toy soldiers, a tattered flag, Confederate money, and old newspapers and photographs had rotted into one giant mess of mush that looked like a "mummified alien." So they froze it, then put the whole mess in a glass case at the museum!

Radical Recycling

Put your poop, pee, and other yuckables to good use! Here are a few ways to turn gross stuff into good stuff:

I Can Pee Clearly Now

In colonial times in America, rags dipped in pee were used to clean windows.

Romans used crushed mouse brains for toothpaste, and they gargled with pee.

The Buzz

Stinky socks are helping to fight malaria, a deadly disease spread by the bite of infected mosquitos. How? Scientists have learned that mosquitoes like stinky-sock smell even more than the smell of blood, so they've begun to trap malaria-carrying mosquitoes using old smelly socks as bait.

Bacteria Busters!

Doctors in the U.K. use maggots to speed up healing a wound, ulcer, or burn. The maggots picnic on pus that can make the wound infected.

Pee You!

Three, Two, One, blast off! You're in outer space, and you're thirsty. Whadda ya do? Have a glass of pee. A water purifier at the International Space Station turns sweat and pee into drinking water.
Thirsty, anyone?

Fish Eat Dandruff?

In Japan, instead of a spa treatment, you can dip into a pool of hungry carp. Nibble, nibble. The fish will eat away your dry, scaly, flaky skin.

Move Over, Green — Go Brown!

Would you live in a house made of poop?

In Indonesia, there's a lot of cow dung. But it's being made into bricks that are lighter and stronger than clay bricks.

This Bus Runs on Poop!

From potty to power, a year's worth of your poop can be turned into 2.1 gallons of usable diesel fuel.

Lifesaver

The Incas are famous for building Machu Picchu, a city high up in the Andes Mountains. But they could not have done it without poop. What? That's right. Llama dung fertilized the soil so that corn could grow at super-high altitudes.

Save a Tree!

Use paper made of elephant poop. No lie.
Elephants are vegetarians, so their poop
has a lot of fiber—the same stuff used to
make paper. It's fragrance free, too!

- Elephants eat
  250 kilograms
  of food
  per day.

- An elephant
  poops about
  50 kilograms
  of dung
  a day.

- From that,
  115 sheets
  of paper can
  be made.

Happy Mother's Day!

Is your mom pooped out? Tweet your mother to a very special facial—with a Japanese face cream that contains bird poop. Yes, nightingale poop facials are all the rage in Japan for smooth skin.

Unhappy Meal?

Scientist Mitsuyuki Ikeda has taken protein from human poop and made it into meat. Nickname: the poop burger. *Got ketchup?*

Potty Potty

Virginia Gardiner has come up with a waterless, flushless, odorless toilet made out of . . . horse manure.

A Car that Smells like French Fries?

Leftover French fry oil can be converted to power a car. Prince Charles of England has a train that runs completely off of the stuff. *How about some fish to go with those chips?*

Annual Stink-O Fests

Feel a booger coming on? April 23 is International Nose Picking Day. (And while you're at it, September 8 is Nose Hair Maintenance Day.)

Enter your smelly sneakers in the National Odor-Eaters Rotten Sneaker Contest in Montpelier, Vermont. If your sneakers outstink all the others, you win $2,500 and a spot in the "Hall of Fumes"!

Head to Talkeetna, Alaska, for the Annual Moose Dropping Festival. Moose turds are dropped from a helicopter, and festivalgoers bet on whether they will hit a target. A pancake breakfast, parade, and moose-poop toss are all part of the two-day fun.

Hail to the toilet! January 27 is Thomas Crapper Day, a day to honor the guy who invented the flush toilet.

Gross Gags and P.U. Pranks

Liven up the sleepover! Freak out your favorite friend or sister.

A Tube of Goo

When your sister, brother, parent, or friend isn't looking, empty out half of the toothpaste from a tube.

Replace it with something gross such as chocolate pudding or apple juice. Screw the lid back on, and wait innocently for the next person to brush his or her teeth.

Make Fake Bird Poop!

You will need:
- 1 cup whipped cream
- 1/4 cup black pepper

Place the whipped cream into a mixing bowl. Mix the pepper into the whipped cream with a spoon or whisk.

If you have a turkey baster, it's a great way to suck up some of the fake poop, then squeeze it onto the hood of your dad's car, a door handle, your sister's backpack, or wherever you want to play the prank.

A Classic:
The Fake Fly in the Ice Cube

Drop one of these cubes in
a glass of ice water when
your friend isn't looking.

How About the Old Vaseline
on the Doorknob Trick?

Spread a little petroleum jelly on a doorknob,
then wait for it . . . "Groooossss!"

Hey, Scab Face!

Wait till your brother or sister falls asleep. Use face paint to draw scabs or use toothpaste to make boogers on them! Quick, hide the mirror!

Take the Stink-y Trivia Challenge!

1. What gross club does Stink's sister, Judy, trick him into joining?
   a. the Bug Eaters Club
   b. the Toad Pee Club
   c. the Smelly Sneaker Siblings Society

2. Stink hopes to get a whiff someday of something super-stinky. It's taller than a man, smells worse than roadkill, and is the color of blood. What is it?
   a. a corpse flower
   b. a sweaty hippo
   c. Bigfoot

3. When Stink's friend Sophie of the Elves dresses up as a zombie, what kind of zombie is she?
   a. a zombie cheerleader
   b. a zombie Girl Scout
   c. a zombie unicorn

4. What smelly job does Stink wish he could do someday?
   a. roadkill scooper-upper
   b. whale-poop collector
   c. professional smeller for NASA

5. What body part belonging to Stink does Judy take to school in a jar for Sharing Day?
   a. some earwax
   b. his baby belly button
   c. some toenail clippings

6. Where does Astro the guinea pig hide in Stink's room?
   a. in his underwear drawer
   b. in his smelly sneaker
   c. in his trash can

7. What yucky disease does Stink think he has on the ferry boat to Artichoke Island?
   a. anchovy
   b. Harvey's curse
   c. scurvy

8. When Judy is having a Bummer Summer at the UN-Zone, something yucky gets into Stink's sandwich. What is it?
   a. elephant snot
   b. slug slime
   c. Bigfoot scat

9. Stink's mom teaches him another name for perfume. What is it?
   a. toilet water
   b. poop juice
   c. eau de foulette

10. When the Zombie Lunch Lady takes over the cafeteria, what does she serve for lunch?
    a. eyeball soup
    b. zombie fried rice
    c. sloppy toes on a bun
    d. all of the above

11. In *Stink and the World's Worst Super-Stinky Sneakers*, he learns that a scientific term for skunk spray is:
    a. *Stinconium de pu*
    b. C_4H_9SeH
    c. musqackia

Turn to page 119 for the answers.

Gross ... Grosser ... Grossest!

Would you rather get grossed out?
Or play the gross-out version of
the Would You Rather game?

Read the questions below aloud
and quiz your friends.

Have a disgusting time!

WOULD YOU RATHER ...
Live in a house made of dinosaur dung?
OR
Camp in a tent made of dead skunk skins?

WOULD YOU RATHER ...
Dive into a pool of hippo pee?
OR
Swim in a lake of fish eyes?

WOULD YOU RATHER . . .
Be nicknamed Benjy Boogerbrain?
OR
Be nicknamed Pickles Poopypants?

WOULD YOU RATHER . . .
Drink a maggot milk shake?
OR
Eat chocolate-covered tarantulas?

WOULD YOU RATHER . . .
Have a pet Tasmanian devil that
reeks of death and decay?
OR
Have a pet zorilla (striped polecat)
that is so stinky it can be smelled
from half a mile away?

WOULD YOU RATHER . . .
Smell a corpse flower?
OR
Smell *like* a corpse flower?

WOULD YOU RATHER . . .
Wear a beard of bees?
OR
Take a bath in poison ivy?

WOULD YOU RATHER . . .
Get caught in a centipede snowstorm?
OR
Dig your way out of a booger blizzard?

WOULD YOU RATHER . . .
Be sprayed by a skunk?
OR
Be spit on by a camel?

WOULD YOU RATHER . . .
Go years without taking a bath?
OR
Take a bath in blood?

WOULD YOU RATHER . . .
Be covered with pig grease?
OR
Be covered with bird poop?

WOULD YOU RATHER . . .
Pick out and eat food from between a
crocodile's teeth?
OR
Collect and eat the gunk from an
elephant's eyes?

WOULD YOU RATHER . . .
Brush your teeth with crushed mouse brains?
OR
Brush your teeth with cow poop?

Selected Sources

The Bathroom Readers' Institute. *Uncle John's Creature Feature Bathroom Reader for Kids Only!* Ashland, OR: Portable Press, 2010.

Borgenicht, David, Nathaniel Marunas, and Robin Epstein. *Worst-Case Scenario Survival Handbook: Gross Junior Edition.* Worst-Case Scenario Survival Handbooks. Illustrated by Chuck Gonzales. San Francisco: Chronicle, 2010.

Branzei, Sylvia. *Grossology: The Science of Really Gross Things.* Illustrated by Jack Keely. New York: Price Stern Sloan, 2002.

Connolly, Sean. *The Book of Totally Irresponsible Science: 64 Daring Experiments for Young Scientists.* New York: Workman, 2008.

Dobson, Mary. *Reeking Royals.* Smelly Old History series. New York: Oxford University Press, 1999.

Glenday, Craig, ed. *Guinness World Records 2011.* New York: Bantam, 2011.

Hargrave, Sir John. *Sir John Hargrave's Mischief Maker's Manual.* New York: Grosset and Dunlap, 2009.

MacDonald, Guy. *Even More Children's Miscellany: Smart, Silly, and Strange Information That's Essential to Know.* Illustrated by Niki Catlow. San Francisco: Chronicle, 2008.

Masoff, Joy. *Oh, Yikes! History's Grossest, Wackiest Moments.* Illustrated by Terry Sirrell. New York: Workman, 2006.

———. *Oh, Yuck! The Encyclopedia of Everything Nasty.* Illustrated by Terry Sirrell. New York: Workman, 2000.

National Children's Book and Literacy Alliance. *The Exquisite Corpse Adventure.* Somerville, MA: Candlewick Press, 2011.

Ramos-Elorduy, Julieta. *Creepy Crawly Cuisine: The Gourmet Guide to Edible Insects.* Photographs by Peter Menzel. Rochester, VT: Park Street Press, 1998.

Szpirglas, Jeff. *They Did What?!: Your Guide to Weird and Wacky Things People Do.* Illustrated by Dave Whamond. Toronto: Maple Tree Press, 2005.

Answers

p. 8–9: Every Breath You Take
1c, 2b, 3c, 4befj, 5h

p. 23: Which Slimeball Said What?
1f, 2g, 3d, 4b, 5c, 6e, 7a

p. 66: Today's Specials!
All true.

p. 89: Test Your Cockroach Know-How
1b, 2c, 3a, 4c, 5b, 6c

pp. 110–113: Take the Stink-y Trivia Challenge!
1b, 2a, 3b, 4c, 5b, 6a, 7c, 8c, 9a, 10d, 11b

Hints

p. 50: Book Cooties
Ginger Pye: Take a peek at "Pyes and Pets."
Mitch and Amy: Don't quarrel looking for Chapter 3!

BE SURE TO CHECK OUT ALL OF STINK'S ADVENTURES!

Stink and the Ultimate Thumb-Wrestling Smackdown
Megan McDonald illustrated by Peter H. Reynolds

Stink and the Midnight Zombie Walk
Megan McDonald illustrated by Peter H. Reynolds

Stink and the Freaky Frog Freakout
Megan McDonald illustrated by Peter H. Reynolds

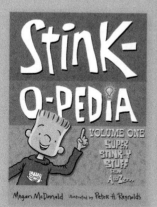

Stink-O-Pedia
VOLUME ONE
SUPER STINKY STUFF from A to Zzzzz

Megan McDonald illustrated by Peter H. Reynolds

Stink-O-Pedia
VOLUME TWO
MORE STINKY STUFF FROM A to Z

Megan McDonald illustrated by Peter H. Reynolds